Rev Up Your Writing in Blogs

BY LISA OWINGS • ILLUSTRATED BY MERNIE GALLAGHER-COLE

Published by The Child's World®
1980 Lookout Drive • Mankato, MN 56003-1705
800-599-READ • www.childsworld.com

ACKNOWLEDGMENTS
The Child's World®: Mary Berendes, Publishing Director
Red Line Editorial: Editorial direction and production
The Design Lab: Design

PHOTOGRAPHS ©: Shutterstock Images, 6, 8 (top), 8 (bottom), 12, 20 (top), 20 (bottom); Zhanna Smolyar/ Shutterstock Images, 14 (top); Daniela Pelazza/ Shutterstock Images, 14 (middle); Olesya Kuznetsova/ Shutterstock Images, 14 (bottom); Tyler Olson/Shutterstock Images, 18

ISBN 9781634070614
LCCN 2014959937

Printed in the United States of America
Mankato, MN
July, 2015
PA02261

ABOUT THE AUTHOR

Lisa Owings has a degree in English and creative writing from the University of Minnesota. She has written and edited a wide variety of educational books for young people. Lisa lives in Andover, Minnesota, with her husband. She very much enjoys reading blogs, especially when they are about food.

ABOUT THE ILLUSTRATOR

Mernie Gallagher-Cole is a children's book illustrator living in West Chester, Pennsylvania. She loves drawing every day. Her illustrations can also be found on greeting cards, puzzles, e-books, and educational apps.

Table of Contents

CHAPTER ONE

Welcome to the Blogosphere

Having a place to express yourself can be wonderful. You might keep a journal to write about your experiences. Or perhaps you write stories, poems, or songs. Many people like to jot down ideas. Maybe you collect pictures, quotes, or other things that inspire you.

Or you might prefer to keep notes about your **hobbies** and interests.

Blogs give you a space to do all of these things. And you do not even have to hunt down a pen and paper. Blogs also make it easy to share your ideas with others.

So what is a blog, anyway? *Blog* is short for *weblog*. The *web* part means a blog is posted on the Web. Other Internet users can read and comment on blogs. That means blogs are great for sharing and discussing your writing with others. But a blog can also be just for you.

Most blogs are not private like journals or diaries. So it is important to think about what you want to share with the world.

The *log* part means a blog is a record of thoughts or events. Think of it like a journal. Each blog entry shows the date it was posted. And a blog is not complete with just one entry. Most people write new posts regularly.

All blogs are set up in a similar way. Each has its own Web site. You can share your blog with friends by telling them your Web address. When they go online and type it in, they will see your blog's name at the top of the page.

The name can look fancy or simple. The important thing is that it hints at what your blog is all about.

Under your blog's name is your newest post. It will have its own title. It will also have a date. Under that comes the text you wrote that day and any images you added. At the bottom of the post is a place for people to leave comments. From there, readers can scroll down to see older posts.

Max's Awesome Adventures

September 5

My New Best Friend

I have wanted a dog forever. Well, the day is finally here! My parents took me to the adoption center. At first I was sad because they did not have any puppies. But then I realized the older dogs were cool, too. One of them ran up and licked my face. Then she let me rub her belly. She was really nice and playful. I begged Mom and Dad to let me take her home. They talked to one of the ladies at the center for a long time. Then they said we were keeping her!

We named our dog Penny. She loves playing fetch and riding in the car. She is already trained. I get to walk her every day after school. Penny is really cute. I will post more pictures of her later. Right now I am going to play with my new best friend.

1 comment
She is so cute! Can't wait to meet her!

September 1

Starting Our Garden

...

QUESTION
Find the date, title, and comment section of this blog post. What types of posts do you think Max likes to write?

CHAPTER TWO

Blogging for Yourself

Your blog should be for you, especially in the beginning. Try not to think about what others want to read. Think about what *you* want to write. Your blog should be about you and your interests. Being excited about what you write makes blogging fun.

Some **bloggers** write whatever they feel in the moment. Others like to stick with an overall **theme**. Most blogs are **nonfiction**. But they have plenty of personal thoughts thrown in.

Do you have an idea of what you want to blog about? Great! The next step is setting up your blog. Ask a parent or teacher to help you create one online. You can do this for free on many sites. Change the **settings** on your blog to make it private. This way, only you can see what you post. You can always share your blog later on.

Not sure where to start? Try writing about your daily life. Or discuss some of your favorite places. You could also write about a hobby.

First you will need a name for your blog. Choose one that hints at what your blog is about. Try to keep it short and snappy. If you later choose to share your blog, this will help others remember its name.

Now comes the fun part. You get to start posting. You might want to post a new recipe, poem, or picture every day. Or you can add more variety. You could describe an important event in your life. You could write about a book or Web site that interests you. Another idea is to tell how to do something step by step. You can also write a **review**. In fact, there is almost no limit to what you can write. Be creative!

Brushes with Greatness

December 7

Winter Wonderland

It is so cold outside! All I want to do is stay indoors and paint. The snow this morning was beautiful, though. I went out and took some pictures before it melted. Then I tried to paint a winter wonderland.

It was hard to make the snow look realistic. But I am pretty happy with how the painting turned out. I plan to hang it up for the holidays.

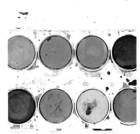

December 1

Favorite Paints

Choosing paints can be hard. I have tried acrylic, watercolor, and oil paints. Watercolors are my favorite. I love their soft look. I also like how the colors flow together.

I really enjoy my Solara watercolor paints. The colors are great. And they are not too expensive. They come in tubes and are easy to mix. I am saving up to get the pro series. I can't wait to see how they compare.

November 29

10 Painting Techniques to Try

...

CHAPTER THREE

Sharing with Others

Are you interested in sharing your blog? Ask your parents for permission first. If they say yes, keep a few things in mind. Never post personal information on your blog. That includes your full name, phone number, and address. Talk to your parents before posting pictures of

yourself or others. And never meet up with anyone you do not know in real life.

Next, think about your **audience**. Will it be family and friends? Teachers and classmates? Anyone who finds your blog online? Most blogging sites let you share your blog with only certain people. Think about your audience as you write. What do you want them to know about? What would you prefer to keep private?

Make your blog easy and fun to read. Create short, descriptive titles for your posts. Take your time writing

As time goes on, you will get better at blogging. You may find yourself posting more often. You can look back at old posts to see how you have improved.

each entry. Then go back and edit. Make sure your post says what you want it to say. Correct any errors and keep things **concise**. Images can help draw readers into your posts. You can use your own images or give **credit** to others.

The **blogosphere** is a big place. Think about how you can make your blog stand out. Try reading other blogs like yours. Does your blog offer something different? You might have a hobby or interest that few others have written about. Maybe your writing style is funny or poetic. Or perhaps you take amazing photos that look nothing like anyone else's. Your blog is a space to show off your unique strengths.

However you use your blog, have fun with it. Stay true to yourself. And keep posting!

You Know It: The Student Council Blog

April 10

Help Plan the Library!

In case you have not heard, our school is getting a new library next year. The student council is helping with the plan. We are asking for more computers and a larger reading area. But we want your feedback, too. What would you like to see in our new library? Please comment below with your ideas.

4 comments

Rocio
I think we should have a bigger science fiction section. The books I want are always checked out.

Tyler
Comfier sofas would be great.

Quinn
Is everything going to be different? I like our library the way it is.

> *You Know It*
> *Quinn, not everything will be different. We will still have all the same books and the same basic layout. And the same librarians. The new library will just be a bit bigger and nicer.*

March 26

No More Bullying

...

TIPS FOR YOUNG WRITERS

1. Brainstorm names for your blog. Then ask friends and family for feedback.

2. Blog about what interests you most.

3. Reread each blog entry before you post it. Find at least one thing to correct or improve.

4. Keep your blog posts as concise as possible.

5. Post often. The more you write, the better your writing will get.

6. Bored of blogging? Write a different type of post or try out a new style.

7. Never post personal information on your blog. Keep information about people you know private, too.

8. Be respectful when commenting on others' blogs.

9. Ask for advice and ideas from your readers and other bloggers.

10. Look back on old posts to see how far your writing has come.

GLOSSARY

audience *(AW-dee-uhns):* An audience is the people who read your writing. Keep your audience in mind when writing your blog.

bloggers *(BLAWG-uhrz):* Bloggers are people who write blogs, or online journals. You can learn a lot from other bloggers.

blogosphere *(BLAWG-uhs-feer):* The blogosphere is made up of all the blogs online. Your blog is part of the blogosphere.

concise *(kuhn-SISE):* Concise means giving a lot of information in just a few words. Blog posts should be concise.

credit *(KRED-it):* To give someone credit for something means to let others know who made or did it. Be sure to give others credit if you use their images or ideas on your blog.

hobbies *(HAH-beez):* Hobbies are things you do for fun. Writing and painting are common hobbies.

nonfiction *(non-FIK-shun):* Nonfiction is writing about things that are true. Most blog entries are nonfiction.

review *(ri-VYOO):* A review is a piece of writing that gives an opinion about an item or event. Product reviews and book reviews are common blog posts.

settings *(SET-ingz):* Settings are preferences about how your blog is set up. You can change the settings on your blog at any time.

theme *(THEEM):* A theme is the main subject or idea behind a blog. On a blog that has a food theme, you might post recipes.

TO LEARN MORE

BOOKS

Jakubiak, David J. *A Smart Kid's Guide to Social Networking Online*. New York: PowerKids Press, 2010.

Mazer, Anne, and Ellen Potter. *Spilling Ink: A Young Writer's Handbook*. New York: Roaring Book Press, 2010.

StJohn, Amanda. *Bridget and Bo Build a Blog*. Chicago: Norwood House Press, 2012.

ON THE WEB

Visit our Web site for lots of links about blogs:
www.childsworld.com/links

Note to Parents, Teachers, and Librarians: We routinely check our Web links to make sure they're safe, active sites—so encourage your readers to check them out!

INDEX